Exploring Denmark

Fascinating Facts for Young Learners.

By Author Jamie Pedrazzoli

All rights reserved, Copyright 2023© by Jamie Pedrazzoli AKA Author Jamie Bach

Copyright fuels creativity. Thank you for buying an authorized edition of this book and complying with the copyright laws by not reproducing, scanning, or distributing any part of this book in any form without permission. To contact the author for permissions email **pedrazzolij@yahoo.com.**

ISBN: 9798396974890

This book is dedicated to my beautiful daughters.

Remember if you wish to contact this author an email address is provided. Do not call her or her parents' home. This is an invasion of privacy and is not appreciated. If it is of urgent importance EMAIL is the best way.

That email is **pedrazzolij@yahoo.com**

Check out her website and other links to social media.

Author site on Facebook

https://www.facebook.com/jamiebachauthorchildrensbooks

Author sites

http://authorjamiebach.weebly.com

http://zolibooks.weebly.com

Twitter

https://twitter.com/jamiebach421

Adventure Blog

http://theadventuresofkobyjackandbogart.weebly.com

Instagram

https://www.instagram.com/jamiepedrazzoliauthor

http://www.instagram.com/jamiebach421author

About the Author

Jamie Pedrazzoli (Jamie Bach) grew up in Vero Beach Florida where she spent time taking art classes in high school with the Center for the Arts Museum. She enjoys reading and writing.

She has three daughters that help inspire her to write.

"I'm so glad I can share my books with the world; I hope everyone enjoys reading them".

For Adults or Teens

Aleida Orphan no more a Cinderella story with a twist

Words of encouragement and how to cope with what life brings you

Untrusting Eyes

School for the Enchanted

Please support me as an author by checking out my other books available under Jamie Bach. My books can be purchased online at most online bookstores.

For kids and young adults

Tongue-twisting alphabet fun with Koby Jack and Bogart

Counting shapes and color fun with Koby Jack and Bogart

My Jungle Adventure in Costa Rica

Jess the Fox (also in Spanish) Jess el Zorro

Florida girls

Florida girls 2

Let's learn sight words Kindergarten

Disclaimer: LEGO is a trademark of the LEGO Group of companies that do not sponsor, authorize, or endorse this book. They were mentioned in this book to give information on where the product came from.

Other books in this series include:

Exploring Romania

Exploring Ireland

Exploring Costa Rica

Exploring New Zealand

Exploring Germany

Exploring Zambia

Exploring Mexico

Exploring Japan

Exploring the Philippines

Exploring India

Exploring South Africa

Exploring Jordan

Exploring Ukraine

There is a list of 7,000 names that parents can choose from when naming a child. If they want a name that is not on the list, they must get permission from the local church and government officials.

There are two official National Anthems.

Øresund (ew-wer-son) Bridge is 5 miles long and connects Denmark to Sweden.

It gets dark by 3 pm on the island of Bornholm.

The Marguerite Daisy is the National Flower.

Thank you for letting me speak to you about my country, Farewell, or Farvel (far-vel).

The End.

Gudenå (goo-nyuh) is the longest river in Denmark.

JØrn Utzon is a famous Danish architect who designed the Sydney Opera House in Australia.

Kronborg Castle was the model for William Shakespeare's play Hamlet.

Here is the Kronborg Castle behind us in this photo.

**

Here are some fast facts about the Kingdom of Denmark.

The curved Lur horn is the oldest musical instrument found in Denmark.

Three letters in the Danish alphabet are not in the English alphabet. They are vowels and come after the letter Z. They are Æ, Ø, and Å.

No place in Denmark is more than one hour's drive from the sea.

Let's speak about some sports we like to play and watch here in Denmark. The national sport is Football, or in American English, Soccer. Our National Soccer team is called the Danish Dynamite.

People here like to ride four-wheelers, play badminton, do gymnastics, swim, windsurf, canoe, and fish.

The Folketing is made up of 178 members, including two from Greenland, and two from the Faroe Islands.

The Prime Minister must have support from the Folketing. About 20 more ministers run the departments of government such as Justice, Finance, and Agriculture, and make up the cabinet.

Queen Margrethe II has been on the throne for over forty years!

Norway was ruled by Denmark until 1814.

In 1849 a Democratic Constitution was adopted and gave power to a Bicameral Parliament.

From 1914 to 1945 Denmark remained neutral in World War I and World War II.

In 1953 we abolished the Upper House of Parliament and allowed women to have a succession to the throne.

In 1970 Denmark faced economic hard times.

In 1972 the people voted to become a member of the European Economic Community (EEC) now known as the European Union (EU).

What is the Danish Government like?

Denmark's government is a Constitutional Monarchy. It is made of the Legislative, Executive, and Judicial branches.

Legislative power is in the Sovereign, Monarch, and Unicameral Parliament called the Folketing.

Now I want to tell you a little bit about Danish History.

The word Viking is believed to come from the Old Norse word Vik, which means creek.

Vikings were sea warriors from the bays and inlets of Scandinavia. From 793 to 1066 AD the Danish Vikings sailed the seas; this was known as the Age of the Vikings! They were feared throughout Europe and were known to trade goods, raid places, and go on conquests.

Some of my favorite foods are SmØrrebrØd (shmal-bod) and HakkebØf. (Hak-e-boof)

My favorite SmØrrebrØd is a piece of buttered rye bread, with meat, cucumber, and eggs. They can be made in many ways and are the best sandwiches in the world to me!

HakkebØf is ground beef with fried onions.

Meatballs are delicious and a common meal here!

Lamb is a delicacy and is very expensive so I usually get that on my birthday or for a rare treat.

Of course, Denmark is known for its Danishes! They come in different varieties. A buttery crust with cream cheese and dried fruit is my favorite type!

Denmark has high taxes but in return, free healthcare, hospitalization, and pensions are given to the elderly over the age of 65.

We believe no citizen should suffer any hardship. We have free education, unemployment, housing allowance, child services, and child support.

My family gets a check for me until I turn eighteen.

Natural resources are limited here but we produce enough oil and gas to satisfy energy requirements in our country and we are trying to teach the rest of the world how to save and conserve their energy.

In 1980 windmills or turbines were developed to use the western winds. Wind power has become a big business here. It produces 13% of our electricity!

We have also been experimenting with electric cars!

Off the Northern Coast, I have seen Beluga whales! They are white with large bumps on their heads that remind me of melons. I heard they weigh up to 1,500 Kg or 3,000 lbs!

There was a problem with overfishing in the 1980s, however, new laws have helped stop that problem.

More than 300 species of birds can be seen in Denmark. I like to go birdwatching with my family.

The National bird is the Mute Swan.

There are only two types of lizards in Denmark. They are the sand lizard and the common lizard.

There are many different frogs, toads, and salamanders here.

Forests cover ten percent of the country. Some of the trees that make up the forests are spruce, fir, beech, oak, elm, and linden.

Some animals you may find in the forests are roe deer, red deer, hares, foxes, squirrels, hedgehogs, European polecats, and bears. Sadly, most of the larger wildlife has died off.

We have farms here with chickens, sheep, ducks, pigs, and dairy cows.

Some crops produced on our farms are cereal, wheat, and barley.

Many people farm part-time or as a hobby. Some people from the cities buy a plot of land and come here to grow things. The most popular meat in Denmark is pork, so there are a lot of pig farms in Denmark.

We have the Dyrenes Verden Filskov Mini Zoo. Here you will find the biggest bird cage in Denmark! There are also kangaroos, small monkeys, and foxes.

The Billund Kommunes Museer is a living museum! People get to see what it is like working in agriculture. This museum is surrounded by moors and meadows.

My family likes to walk around Skulpturpark and look at the artwork. Here is a photo of me and my twin sister Laura in front of our favorite sculpture.

There are also a lot of hiking trails here. People love to spend time outdoors in these areas.

What else is there to do in my town?

There are many churches and cathedrals here that people like to visit.

We have a Teddy Bear Art Museum.

My favorite place to go is Lalandia. It is a waterpark! Does this look fun?

My name is Mikkel.

I live in Billund Denmark. What is so special about where I live? Can you guess by looking at my picture?

The Danish people invented LEGO® blocks! The original Legoland ®theme park opened on June 7, 1968, and it is here in Billund!

The park is located next to the original LEGO ® factory. Legoland® has rides and exhibits made of Legos®. It gets over 1 million visitors every year! The word Lego comes from the words 'Leg Godt' (lie got), which means 'play well'.

Thanks for listening to me speak about Denmark. I will leave you with a few Danish words to learn. Farewell or Farvel (far-vell) from Copenhagen.

Vi Ses (vee-sees) See you soon.

Hej, Jeg Hedder ... (Hi-Yee Hel-der) Hi, my name is ...

Goddag (goo-day) Good day.

Godaften (goo ahf ten) Good afternoon.

Hvordan GÅr det (Vor-den Gor Det) Hows it going?

Det GÅr godt, tak (Det gor got tahk) I'm good thanks.

Farvel (Fahr Vell) Goodbye.

The Festival of Whitsun is celebrated by us welcoming spring with a picnic.

May 5th is Denmark's Liberation Day. We place candles in the windows in remembrance.

In July/ August music festivals are held.

In September in the town of Arhus, they celebrate a Viking Festival!

In November we celebrate All Saints Day. It is usually the First Sunday in November. We remember the dead saints by placing candles on graves.

Before I go, I want to tell you a little more about the different holidays that are celebrated in Denmark.

We celebrate New Year's Day, Valentine's Day, Easter, April Fool's Day, Mother's Day, International Worker's Day, and Queen Margrethe's Birthday.

We celebrate Shrovetide (shrove-tide). This is a children's festival. We dress up in costumes and bring tins around and knock on neighbors' doors and ask them to fill our tins with money.

We also ask for candy and this holiday is sometimes called Fastelavn (fayst-lav).

Risalamande, (Ris-el-la-mond) is a dessert that tastes like vanilla; it is a pudding, and hidden inside is an Almond. Whoever gets this almond wins a special gift! We usually keep it a secret until everyone is finished eating and then we say who has it. I got the almond last year! The gift you receive is decided by family traditions. I got chocolate.

After eating we then exchange and open our gifts.

We usually visit extended family or friends on Christmas Day and have a large lunch.

Some Christmas foods we eat are:

Roast pork, duck, or stuffed goose.

Red cabbage, beets, cranberry jam, and caramelized potatoes.

Brawn, which is boiled meat with soup poured over it.

Brune Kager (broon –care) gingerbread.

Klejner, (kline-er) knotted fried dough.

PebernØdder, (pebber-nodder) or spiced cookies.

We attend a Christmas mass at church where we sing Christmas songs to help us get into the Holiday Spirit. Then we go home to have a large feast.

When the main celebration takes place, we decorate the tree together. We dance around the tree singing, Nu er det jul igen, (new air det Yool ee-in) 'Now it's Christmas time' while holding hands.

This is my little cousin, Vilma decorating the tree.

The Advent Calendar also called a Christmas Calendar has 24 small doors and when we open each door there is usually a small gift or piece of candy hiding inside!

On Christmas Eve, which is December 24th, we walk to the park and feed the animals we see. We do this because it was believed that animals could talk on this one special night. We feed them so they say good things about us. It is silly but fun.

Lucia (loo-che-uh) Night is named after Saint Lucia or the Saint of Light. She is celebrated on the night between the 12th and 13th of December.

Some Christmas traditions we do here are lighting the Advent Wreath and opening the Advent Calendar.

The Advent Wreath has four candles in it and we light one every Sunday leading up to Christmas to celebrate the birth of baby Jesus. The wreath was traditionally made from Spruce twigs and decorated with red ribbons.

I want to share a little about my favorite holiday in Denmark.

Can you guess which one it is? If you guessed Jul (yool) or Christmas you are right!

The entire month of December is celebrated in Denmark. We start on December first. The streets are decorated with lights we call fairy lights. Garlands are hanging on street lamps, wreaths decorating windows, and bells hanging on doors.

In Denmark, we strongly believe in Hygge, (who- gah) which translates to contentment or well-being.

We talk about 'Hygge' when it comes to family. Families are close and spend a lot of time together. We are brought up well-mannered, responsible, and very independent. Most children live with their parents until they reach their mid-20s.

What do you like to do for fun?

I like to watch theater, make crafts, listen to opera, and dance. As a family, we play card games, watch television, and read.

There are many pastimes that families do together here like walking, cycling, hunting, and fishing. We like to visit the beaches, palaces, castles, and go to museums.

My father usually rides us to school on a bicycle cart. Most people in Denmark walk or ride bikes in the city. We do not like harming the environment so we try not to drive cars very much.

Some buses and trains get people where they need to go. Bridges join most of the islands and we have ferry boats that go back and forth.

What is the school like here?

An average school day is from 8 A.M. to 11:30 A.M. Sometimes we stay in aftercare if our parents are working late. We have about 19 students in our class and we go Monday through Friday. Fridays are my favorite because we usually play for most of the day.

There is a huge music festival called Roskilde (Ros-kil-ay) Festival. It goes on for four days in the summer. It is usually held the last weekend of June or the first weekend of July. There are over 150 bands and it is the largest of its kind in Europe.

The Royal Danish Ballet was founded in 1748 and has a troupe of nearly 100 dancers! This is very popular to go and see.

Here I am at Tivoli Gardens. It has an exciting roller coaster. Would you ride it?

Amalienborg is home to the Royal Danish Family and is found here in the capital city.

The Grundtvig Church is known for its unusual appearance and is the best-known church in the city.

There are so many more castles in Denmark; you will have to look them up yourselves! If I keep talking about them, we will be here all day!

The Rosenborg Castle has a beautiful king's garden and is the most popular place to visit in Copenhagen. There is a statue of the famous Hans Christian Anderson.

Who was he? He wrote The Ugly Duckling, The Little Mermaid, and many more stories you may know. In the summer they hold a puppet show here for children and it is a special place for people who like to come to sunbathe.

Copenhagen has many castles and palaces to see.

The Christiansborg Palace is the house of the Danish Parliament, the Prime Minister's Office, and the Supreme Court. There are also rooms here for the royal family.

What is there to see and do in my city?

Copenhagen is known for Tivoli Gardens, which is not only a garden but also a theme park! I enjoy going here with my family.

There is also a statue of the little mermaid that many people like to see. It is made from Bronze Metal.

There she is, the little mermaid statue is behind me.

During June, July, and August the days are long and the sky stays bright late into the night and brightens early in the morning.

I live in the capital city of Denmark, Copenhagen. I live near the famous Nyhavn Harbor.

Ten percent of the country's population lives here. There is an estimated population of 5.8 million in the entire county (2022 report).

Our population consists of Danish, Inuit, and Faroese. The Faroese are descended from the Ancient Vikings!

The land here is low and flat and the coasts are lined with sandy beaches. The islands have rich soil that is good for planting. The Western Coast is not very populated because of the winds and sand dunes. Zealand is the most populated of Denmark's Islands.

Our climate is mild.

Winters can be wet and average 32 degrees Fahrenheit or 0 degrees Celsius. In the summer the average temperature is 61 degrees Fahrenheit or 16 degrees Celsius.

This is a photo of me and my brother Oliver at the Faroe Islands. They are so beautiful.

Denmark is made up of over four hundred islands and is surrounded by the Norwegian and Baltic Sea.

Our money is called the Danish Krone. 6.96 Danish Krone is about 1 USD.

Our flag is called the Danneborg, or Danish Cloth. The Flag of Denmark holds the record for the oldest national flag that is still used today. It is red and white. The red represents the battle and bloodshed of our history, the white cross represents our Christian Heritage, and the holy cause of why the blood was shed.

Hej, (hey) or Hello.

My name is Karla. I am going to tell you about my country. Velkommen, (Vel-come) or Welcome, I am from Denmark.

My country is officially called the Kingdom of Denmark. It is in Northern Europe in an area known as Scandinavia. Denmark also consists of the Faroe Islands and Greenland.

The names in this book are used fictitiously and any resemblance of persons is coincidental. The facts in this book are based on information provided to the author.

I attempted to put the sound of foreign words in parenthesis to help you pronounce them easier.

Please remember that I speak English so I am attempting to help others pronounce the words by the way I hear them.

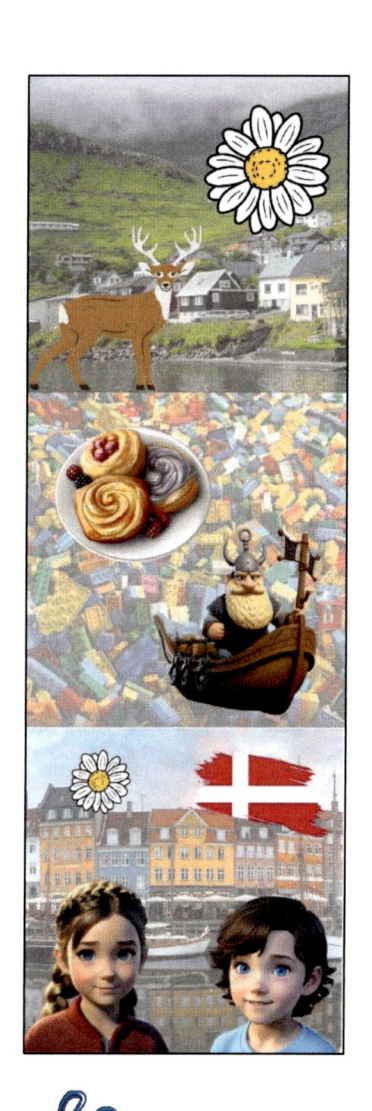

Have an adult help you cut out the collectible bookmark to use while reading this book.

Made in the USA
Las Vegas, NV
30 March 2025